Where We Live

Australia

Donna Bailey and Jean Chapman

STECK-VAUGHN
L I B R A R Y
A Division of Steck-Vaughn Company

Hello! My name is Ken.

I live in Sydney.

Sydney is the biggest city in Australia.

It is built around a natural harbor

which has many bays and inlets.

2

Our house is in North Sydney on
the north shore of Sydney Harbor.
To drive to the business center of Sydney,
we cross over Sydney Harbor Bridge.

When Dad goes to work, he crosses
Sydney Harbor by ferry.
There are ships, sailing boats, and
ferries in the harbor.

Ships come to Sydney from
all over the world.
The docks are always very busy.
Big ships and small ships load and
unload their cargoes.

Many people who live in Sydney
like to sail and swim.
We have our own sailboat, which
we like to sail in the races
in Sydney Harbor.

In Sydney, the summer is warm and sunny.
We spend most of our time outside.
We often have a barbecue in the backyard
or take a picnic down to the beach.

The hottest months of the year are
January and February.
That's when we have our long summer holidays.
We spend a lot of time on the beach then.
We once had Christmas dinner at the beach!

Most Australian children learn to swim
when they are very young.
We have a swimming pool in our backyard.
But it is more fun to go to the beach.
We often go to Manly, our nearest beach.

Sometimes we go to Bondi Beach.
People like to surf there on the big waves
that roll in from the ocean.
Some stand on their surfboards and try
to balance as the waves sweep onto the beach.

10

Many people in Sydney like surfing.
They also play other sports.
My favorite sports are tennis and cricket.
We play cricket and soccer at school.
On Saturdays I go to an athletic club.

One day we went on a trip with our school
to the Opera House.
It is one of the most famous buildings
in Sydney.

At the Opera House, we saw a show about
the early history of Australia.
After that we went to Luna Park.
I rode the big Ferris wheel.

Another school trip was to
the Royal National Park.
It is in the country, not far
from Sydney.
We went there by bus and had a picnic
when we arrived.

The best way to see the animals in the park
is to walk silently through the forest.
If you are very lucky, you might see kangaroos.
Wombats and koalas also live there.
They look like small bears, but they are not.

15

Kangaroos, wombats, and koalas are native
to Australia.
All three animals carry their babies in pouches.
These koalas eat gum leaves and
sleep in the branches of gum trees.
Many interesting animals live in Australia.

Last year, I spent my winter vacation
with my uncle.
He lives in the southern part of Australia.
First we went by plane from Sydney to Adelaide.
The flight took over four hours.
Then we drove to his home near Port Augusta.

Much of south and central Australia
is very hot and dry.
Australians call it the "Outback."
The biggest town in the Outback is
Alice Springs, which is almost
in the center of Australia.

Most of the roads in the Outback
don't have any fences, so wild animals
wander across them.
Many kangaroos and birds called emus are here.
You can even see herds of wild camels.

Kangaroos often get hit by cars on the roads,
so cars have "roo" bars in front of their engines.
The bars protect the engines and lights
if kangaroos suddenly hop into the road.

Many cars and trucks have shields
over their front windows.
The shields protect the windows from stones
that can bounce up and break the windows.

Very large trucks, called road trains,
are used to move goods and cattle
from Alice Springs to the cities.
Road trains often travel together
across the Outback.

Children living in the Outback
don't go to school like other children.
They get their lessons through the mail
every two weeks.
They switch on a special two-way radio at home.
A teacher talks to them over the radio, and
they can talk to the teacher.

People in the Outback use the radio
to talk to each other.
They can ask each other for help
or tell where the kangaroos
have broken down their fences.

24

They also use the radio to call
the "Flying Doctor" service.
The doctor talks over the radio and
tells what should be done for the patient.
Sometimes the doctor flies in to take
the sick person to the hospital.

25

This man has a sheep station in the Outback.
A station is like a ranch.
He has thousands of sheep on his station.
His workers use dogs to find the sheep.
They often ride motorcycles to round them up.

When the sheep have all been rounded up,
shearers come and cut off their wool.
The workers pack the wool into big bales.
They load the bales into trucks that
take the wool to be sold in the cities.

Some of the workers are Aborigines.
Aborigines have lived in Australia
for thousands of years.
Some of them work in the Outback and
have their own cattle stations.

Ayer's Rock, near Alice Springs,
belongs to the Aborigines.
The Aborigines' name for Ayer's Rock is Uluru.
The cave paintings done by Aborigines in
the caves at Uluru are very famous.

There are many caves at Uluru.
Long ago, the Aborigines painted
and drew on cave walls in many
different places in Australia.

Many of these paintings are sacred to them.
Others show how the Aborigines live and
how they feel about the land.
Aborigines also have many stories, dances,
and songs about the animals and land in the Outback.

West of Ayer's Rock there are 28 big
rounded rocks called the Olgas.
The Olgas and Ayer's Rock can be seen
from far away.
Perhaps you will visit them one day.

Index

Reading Consultant: Diana Bentley
Editorial Consultant: Donna Bailey
Supervising Editor: Kathleen Fitzgibbon

Illustrated by Gill Tomblin
Picture research by Suzanne Williams
Designed by Richard Garratt Design

Photographs
Cover: Robert Harding Picture Library
Bruce Coleman: 19 (Melinda Berge), 5 (C. Bingham), 16 (Eric Crichton),
    1 (Fritz Prenzel), 18 (P. R. Wilkinson)
Susan Griggs Picture Agency: 23 (Ted Spiegel)
Robert Harding Picture Library: 10, 12
The Hutchison Library: 17, 21, 26, 27, 28, 30, 31
Christine Osborne: 6, 7, 8, 11, 13
ZEFA: 3, 4, 20, 22, 29, 32

Library of Congress Cataloging-in-Publication Data: Bailey, Donna. [Australia] Australia / Donna Bailey and
Jean Chapman; [illustrated by Gill Tomblin]. p. cm. —(Where we live) Previously published as: We live in
Australia. SUMMARY: Describes the pleasantries of life in Australia's largest city, Sydney, and presents the
more arduous life of the Outback. ISBN 0-8114-2547-9 1. Australia—Social life and customs— Juvenile
literature. [1. Sydney—Description. 2. Australia—Social life and customs.] I. Chapman, Jean. II. Tomblin,
Gill, ill. III. Title. IV. Series. DU107.B28   1990   994—dc20   89-26124   CIP   AC

1 2 3 4 5 6 7 8 9 LB 96 95 94 93 92 91 90